see and say

guarda e parla

regarde et parle

mira y habla

a picture book in four languages

guarda e parla   mira y habla

See and Say

regarde et parle

woodcuts by

antonio frasconi

harcourt, brace & world, inc., new york

para pablo

Uno solo es lo que ves
aunque te parezcan mas que tres.

Since I was brought up in a home where more than one language was spoken, I was given at an early age the knowledge that there is more than one nation and one way of speaking in our world. The idea that there are many nationalities speaking many languages is to me one of the most important for a child to understand.

See and Say has grown from this belief and from my experience and personal need in living with and teaching my son Pablo.

Beside each object pictured in this book you will find the word for it in English, Italian, French, and Spanish, together with a guide to the pronunciation. The following color key has been used throughout: ⚫ Black for English words; 🔵 Blue for Italian words; 🔴 Red for French words; 🟢 Green for Spanish words. There is also a page of everyday expressions all children use.

A.F.

sun
sun

sole
soh-láy

soleil
soh-láy-ee

sol
sohl

chicken
chik-n

poulet
poo-lay

pollo
poh-loh

pollo
poy-oh

tree
tree

albero
áhl-bay-roh

arbre
ahr-br

arbol
áhr-bohl

houses
how-zes

case
kah-zay

maisons
may-zong

casas
kah-sas

egg
eg

uovo
oo-óh-voh

oeuf
uf

huevo
wáy-voh

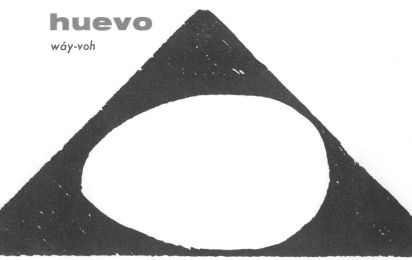

bridge   **ponte**   **pont**   **puent**
brí-j   *póhn-tay*   *pohng*   *pwen-tay*

rose
ro-z

rosa
róh-sah

rose
ro-z

rosa
róh-sah

grasshopper
grás-hop-ur

cavalletta
kah-vahl-lét-tah

sauterelle
soh-te-rél

saltamontes
sal-tah-móhn-tays

suitcase
sóot-kayss

valigia
vah-lée-jah

valise
vah-leess

valija
vah-lée-hah

snail
snayl

lumaca
loo-máh-kah

escargot
es-kar-goh

caracol
kara-kól

bus
bus

autobus
ah'oo-toh-boos

omnibus
ohm-nee-beus

autobus
ah'oo-toh-boos

ants
ants

formiche
for-mée-kay

fourmis
foor-mee

hormigas
or-mée'-gahs

sheep
sheep

pecora
páy-koh-rah

mouton
moo-tóhng

oveja
oh-váy-hah

chair
chair

sedia
sáy-de'ah

chaise
shez

silla
séel-yah

elephant
éle-funt

elefante
ay-lay-fáhn-tay

éléphant
ay-lay-fahng

elefante
ay-lay-fáhn-tay

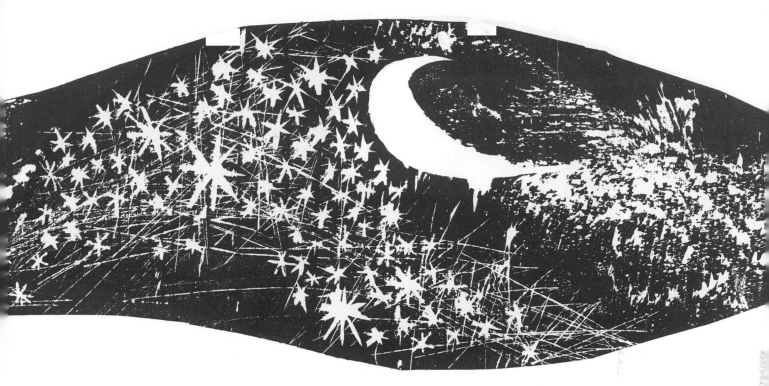

night **notte** **nuit** **noche**
nyt *nóht-tay* *nwee* *nóh-chay*

book
book

libro
lée-broh

livre
lee-vr

libro
lée-broh

corn
kohrn

grano
gráhn-oh

maïs
mah-ées

maiz
mah-éeth

girl
gurl

ragazza
rah-gáht-sah

fille
fee-ee

muchacha
moo-cháh-chah

cow
kow

vacca
vah-kah

vache
vah-sh

vaca
vah-kah

hand   *máhn-oh*   *ma-'ng*   *máhn-oh*

hand   **mano**   **main**   **mano**

barn   **granaio**   **grange**   **granero**

bahrn   *grah-náh-e'oh*   *grahnj*   *grah-náir-oh*

grapes
gráy-pss

uva
óo-vah

raisins
ray-zang

uvas
óoh-vahs

cat
kat

gatto
gah-toh

chat
sha

gato
gah-toh

automobile
áw-toh-moh-beel

automobile
ah'oo-toh-móh-bee-lay

automobile
oh-toh-moh-béel

automóvil
ah'oo-toh-móh-veel

wheel   ruota   roue   rueda

hweel   *roo-óh-tah*   *rooh*   *rwáy-dah*

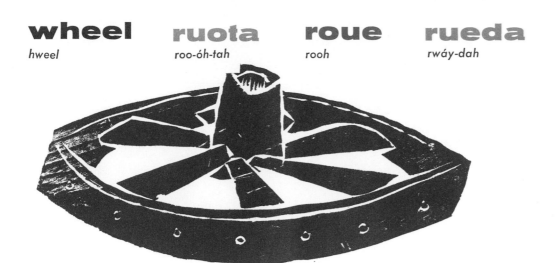

lion   leone   lion   león

ly-on   *lay-óh-nay*   *lee-ohng*   *lay-óhn*

wind   **vento**   **vent**   **viento**

wind   *ven-toh*   *vahng*   *vee-én-toh*

whale

hwayl

balena

bah-láy-nah

baleine

bah-len

ballena

bal-yáy-nah

fishermen
físh-ur-men

pescatori
pess-kah-tóhr-ee

pêcheurs
peh-sheur

pescadores
pess-kah-dór-es

sea
see

mare
máh-ray

mer
mair

mar
mahr

anchor
ánk-or

ancora
ahn-kóh-rah

ancre
ahng-kr

ancla
áhn-klah

Christmas tree
Kris-mus tree

albero di Natale
áhl-bay-roh dee Nah-táh-lay

arbre de Noël
ahr-br duh Noh-el

árbol de Navidad
áhr-bohl day nah-vee-dáhd

tomato
to-máh-toh

pomodoro
poh-moh-doh-roh

tomate
toh-máht

tomate
toh-máh-tay

cake
kayk

torta
tohr-tah

gâteau
ga-toh

torta
tohr-tah

boat
boht

barca
bár-kah

bateau
bah-toh

barco
bar-koh

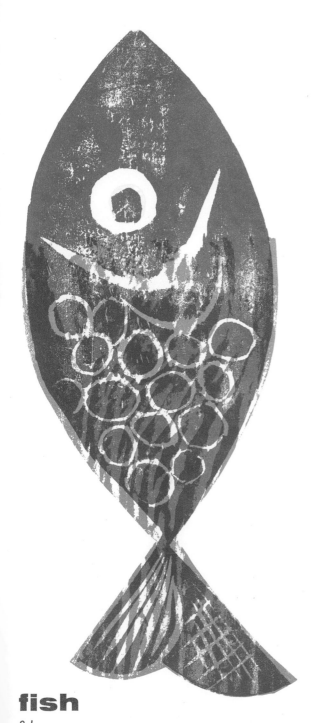

fish
fish

pesce
pé-shay

poisson
pwa-sohng

pescado
pes-káh-doh

hat
hat

cappello
kah-pél-loh

chapeau
sha-póh

sombrero
som-bráir-oh

school
skoohl

scuola
skoo-óh-lah

école
ay-kul

escuela
es-ku-áy-lah

airplane
áir-playn

aeroplano
ah-ay-roh-pláh-noh

aéroplane
air-oh-plan

aeroplano
ah-ay-roh-pláh-noh

horse
hors

cavallo
kah-váhl-loh

cheval
shu-val

caballo
kah-bál-yoh

fly
fly

mosca
mos-kah

mouche
moo-sh

mosca
mos-kah

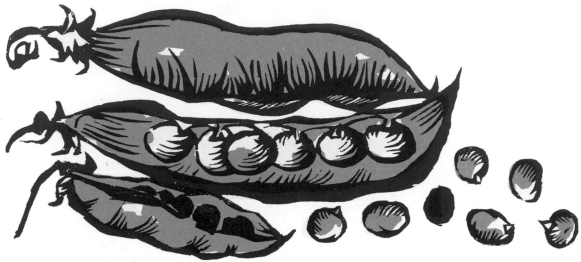

peas   **piselli**   **pois**   **guisantes**
peez   *pee-zél-lee*   *pwah*   *ghee-sán-tays*

dog
dawg

cane
káh-nay

chien
sh'eyng

perro
pér-roh

shoes

shooz

scarpe

skár-pay

souliers

sool-yea

zapatos

thah-páh-tos

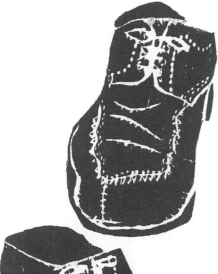

bed

bed

letto

lét-toh

lit

lee

cama

káh-mah

goat
goh-t

capra
kah-prah

chèvre
she-vr

cabra
kah-brah

train
trayn

treno
tráy-noh

train
treyng

tren
trayn

bird
burd

uccello
oo-chéll-oh

oiseau
wah-zóh

pájaro
páh-ha-roh

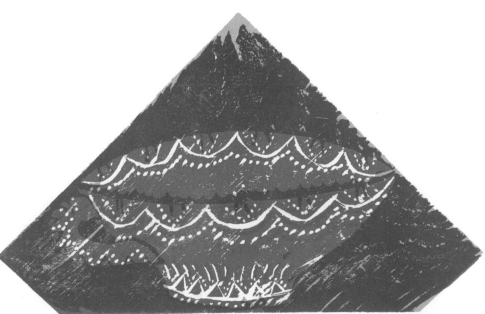

cup
kup

tazza
táht-tsah

tasse
tass

taza
tah-thah

rain
rayn

pioggia
pee-óh-ja

pluie
plwee

lluvia
lyoó-vee-ah

umbrella
um-brél-ah

ombrello
om-brél-oh

parapluie
pah-rah-plwee

paraguas
páh-ráh-gwas

light
lyt

luce
loo-chay

lumière
leum-yair

luz
looth

butterfly
bút-ur-fly

farfalla
far-fáhl-lah

papillon
pah-pee-yong

mariposa
ma-ree-póh-sah

table
tábl

tavola
táh-voh-lah

table
tah-bl

mesa
máy-sah

pig   **porco**   **cochon**   **cerdo**

pig   *por-koh*   *koh-shóng*   *ther-doh*

grass   **erba**   **herbe**   **hierba**

gras   *air-bah*   *air'b*   *yair-bah*

farmer

fár-mur

fattore

fah-tóh-ray

fermier

fair-mee-ay

labrador

lah-brah-dór

turkey

túr-kee

tacchino

tahk-kée-noh

dindon

dehng-dohng

pavo

páhv-oh

world
wuhrld

mondo
món-doh

monde
mohn-d

mundo
mun-doh

clouds
klowd-z

nubi
noo-bee

nuages
neu-ahj

nubes
noo-bes

numbers
núm-burz

numeri
nóo-may-ree

nombres
nohng-br

números
nóo-may-ros

ladder
lad-ur

scala
skáh-lah

échelle
ay-shel

escalera
es-kah-láir-ah

See and Say	Guarda e Parla	Regarde et Parle	Mira y Habla
see and say	*gwar-dah ay par-lah*	*re-gard ay parl*	*mee-rah ee ah-blah*
Happy birthday!	Buon compleanno!	Joyeux Anniversaire!	¡Feliz cumpleaños!
hap-pee burth-day	*bwohn kom-play-áh-noh*	*jwa-euze ah-nee-vair-sair*	*fay-léeth koom-play-áh-nyos*
I love you!	Ti voglio bene!	Je t'aime!	¡Te amo!
i luv yoo	*tee vohl-yoh bay-nay*	*szhuh tem*	*tay áh-moh*
Merry Christmas!	Buon Natale!	Joyeux Noël!	¡Felices Navidades!
máir-ee kris-mus	*bwohn nah-táh-lay*	*jwa-uh noh-él*	*fay-lée-seth nah-vee-dáh-dez*
My name is_____.	Mi chiamo_____.	Je m'appelle_____.	Me llamo_____.
my naym iz	*mee kee-áh-moh*	*szhuh mah-pel*	*may lyáh-moh*
What a beautiful day!	Che bella giornata!	Quelle belle journée!	¡Qué hermoso día!
hwat ay byoo-te-ful day	*kay bél-ah jur-náh-tah*	*kel bel szhur-nay*	*kay air-móh-soh dée-ah*
How are you?	Come stai?	Comment vas-tu?	¿Cómo estás?
how ahr yoo	*koh-may sty*	*koh-mahng vah-too*	*koh-moh ess-táhs*
What are you doing?	Che fai?	Que fais-tu?	¿Qué haces?
hwat ahr yoo doo-ing	*kay fy*	*kuh feh-too*	*kay áh-sess*
Let's have lunch.	Facciamo colazione.	Allons déjeuner.	Vamos a almorzar.
lets hav lunch	*fatch-ee-áh-moh koh-láh-zee-óh-nay*	*a-lohng day-shzeu-nay*	*vah-mohs ah al-mor-zar*
What time is it?	Che ora è?	Quelle heure est-il?	¿Qué hora es?
hwat tym iz it	*kay óh-rah ay*	*kel eur et-teel*	*kay óh-rah ess*
Good morning!	Buon giorno!	Bon jour!	¡Buenos días!
good móhr-ning	*bwohn jor-noh*	*bohng szhuhr*	*bway-nohs dée-ass*
Good night!	Buona notte!	Bonne nuit!	¡Buenas noches!
good nyt	*bwohn-ah noh-tay*	*bun nwee*	*bway-nahs nóh-chess*
Good-bye!	Arrivederci!	Au revoir!	¡Hasta la vista!
good-by	*ah-rée-veh-der-chee*	*oh rev-wahr*	*ah-stah lah vee-stah*
Let's go! 	Andiamo!	Allons!	¡Vámonos!
lets goh	*ahn-dee-áh-moh*	*a-lohng*	*váh-moh-nohs*
Happy New Year!	Buon Anno!	Bonne Année!	¡Feliz Año Nuevo!
hap-pee nyoo yeer	*bwohn ah-noh*	*bun ah-nay*	*fay-leeth ah-nyoh noo-wáy-voh*
That's all.	E questo é tutto.	C'est tout.	Esto es todo.
thats awl	*ay kwes-toh ay too-toh*	*say too*	*ess-toh ess toh-doh*

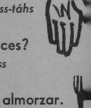
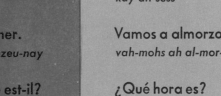